Rejoice in the Lord

Rejoice in the Lord

BRUCE MacDOUGALL

Abingdon/Nashville

Rejoice in the Lord

Copyright © 1979 by Abingdon

Library of Congress Cataloging in Publication Data

MACDOUGALL, BRUCE.
  Rejoice in the Lord.
  1.   Christian life—United Church of Canada authors.
  2.   MacDougall, Bruce.   I.   Title.
  BV4501.2.M228   248'.2[B]   78-10610

ISBN 0-687-35933-3

MANUFACTURED BY THE PARTHENON PRESS AT
NASHVILLE, TENNESSEE, UNITED STATES OF AMERICA

To
Isobel

who has been
a real partner
in the struggle
to be authentic

Contents

Foreword

An interviewer once asked G. P. K. Chesterton what single book he would like to have along if he were stranded on a deserted island. Without hesitation, he said, "A manual on boat building." His nonpious and pragmatic answer indicates the genius of this Christian thinker and writer.

My friend Bruce MacDougall is a writer in the Chesterton tradition. He understands that God is not interested in theology, the Bible is not about religion, the Holy Spirit is not very "spiritual," and that Jesus came to give us life rather than make us good.

One of the main problems with the Christian church today is that the word made flesh has been made word again. By contrast, Bruce MacDougall's refreshing book is a practical approach to "unexpected" changes in life—changes we can all expect if we live long enough. He deals with decision-making, relationships, growing older, sexual confusion, lost identity, missed communication, unexpected failure, false spirituality, role-playing, and all the other trees that make a jungle of our lives. It is so easy to get lost in that jungle.

Well, Bruce MacDougall does not pass out road maps. Rather he notches the trees to let us know that someone has been there before. The notches provide more than comfort in our loneliness and lostness. If we follow them, we might even find our way out. For the reader who wants to learn how to celebrate and affirm life, Bruce is a guide worth following.

Bruce Larson

Introduction

The word that best describes my life these past five years is *change.* But, more than that, my view of what *change* means has altered radically.

I think most Christians have been sold a bill of goods about change, one that is really counter-to-life.

Saint Paul speaks of change in Second Corinthians 3:18 by saying that we are "beholding the glory of the Lord and being changed into his likeness, from one degree of glory to another." I am sure that Paul is speaking the

truth in a poetic sort of way. But the interpreta-
tions of that truth which I have read and which
were given to me never quite *felt* right. They felt
unreal, imaginary, and fanciful. "From one
degree of glory to another" just never felt like it
was or could be a part of my life. I assumed it was
a description of someting very spiritual. It
sounded so mystical, so ethereal, so other-
worldly, so unrelated to my life. It seemed
foreign to where I was and to where others I
knew were. And yet I got the impression that it
described where I should be going.

In retrospect that "other-worldly, ethereal"
interpretation seems strange because in the very
next chapter Paul talks about our having this
treasure in "earthen vessels." Now that is the
kind of language I can understand because it is
down to earth and it speaks to my humanness. It
makes sense to me intellectually and experien-
tially because it acknowledges the reality of my
humanity. I want to suggest that *change for
Christians* is to be understood in the context of
"earthen vessels" rather than in terms of "glory
to glory and other-worldliness." Jesus talked
about change. When He said, "Repent," He was
talking of change. When he told Nicodemus he

must be born again, he was speaking of change. Zacchaeus was invited to change. The woman at the well was confronted with the need to change. But the change of which Jesus spoke seems to be directed to life situations, to where people were. Jesus' call to change is directed to people who are going to express and experience the gospel in the fullness of their humanity. It is change by grace and under grace, but it is experienced in the earthen-vesselled life into which we have been born.

Of course I really believe that Paul too was concerned with change that fully involved our humanity. But for reasons which I do not completely understand, people seem to prefer the glory-to-glory, other-worldly interpretation which contains an implicit put-down of our humanness.

When I shared in some preaching missions in Northern Ontario shortly after ordination, we would give to the new converts a pamphlet which told them what to do after their decision for Christ. Things like: burn your bridges behind you, pray, read your Bible, seek fellowship, and attend church. None of these is wrong, but the total-packaged-message seemed to be that you

13

are now engaged on a journey calculated to move you *away* from your humanity. We seemed to be saying to the new Christians that your decision for Christ would not result in changes to your earthenware humanity, so much as it would take you to a new humanity, a supra-humanity.

If you think I am exaggerating, let me tell you that one night at a training course for telephone workers a visiting expert was asked a question he could not answer. His response was, "Why don't you ask Mr. MacDougall, after all I am only human?" And he was not fooling. He was a churchman who was caught up in the interpretation that Christian change is a beyond-our-humanity trip, and that the clergy were much further on their way than he.

Well, I want to repudiate that plastic, unreal, subhuman concept of change. I believe that the changes of which Paul and Jesus speak are changes that we are called to experience in our full humanity. Changes in the way we see ourselves. Changes in the way in which we relate to and experience others. Paul prefaces his talk about change by saying that where the Lord is, there is freedom. So it seems to me that he is talking about a freedom to change brought about by the presence of the Lord.

This book is about changes I have experienced in the past five years under grace. They are not the kinds of changes I was told by the church to expect or anticipate. I believe they represent some universal aspirations, yearnings, and struggles, and I offer them as an encouragement to others.

Rejoice in the Lord

The Basis of Change

It may seem contradictory, but I want to begin by suggesting that the experiences of change to which we are called must take place in the context of the changelessness of God. The freedom to risk healthy change is possible for me as a Christian because of the constancy, the dependability, and the solidarity of God. The writer to the Hebrews said it: "Jesus Christ is the same yesterday and today and forever" (13:8). It is in this framework that I dare risk change; I know that nothing I risk can separate me from the ever-present grace of God. The constancy of God provides the assurance I need to move.

When I entered the ministry, my father wept. Later I decided to leave the pastorate for the less certain ministry of Faith at Work. He was then convinced that I had taken leave of my senses.

I was sure my father reacted so negatively toward the ministry because he really did not understand, and because he was far less spiritual than I. Since then I have grown up a little, and I think I see more clearly what was happening to my father.

You see, my father was very goal-oriented and security conscious. But, at the age of twenty-five, I had become role-oriented, and hence we could not understand each other. Let me explain.

My father went to work at the age of fifteen. He worked hard and conscientiously, and in the final twelve years of his work he had a very interesting and responsible position representing the railroad to the government in Ottawa. Because he was goal-oriented he worked hard to advance in the company, believing that in the framework of his job he would find himself. In other words, he tried to identify himself in terms of his job, his position, his ambition, his

20

responsibility, his family, and the circumstances of his life.

If you asked him who he was, he would say, "I am Ray MacDougall, Executive Representative of the Canadian National Railway." If you pressed him he would say, "I'm married and I have one son."

As I grew up the question that was constantly being put to me was What are you going to do? And I find myself doing the same with my own children. But you see this is a goal-oriented question. It assumed that I would find myself in the job or the circumstances of the job that I chose. But, like many kids today, I didn't have the slightest clue as to what I wanted to do. I had no goal. So I had no place to find myself. In a sense I was lucky the war came along because I had a second chance to go to school. The only reason I took commerce and later law was because someone said, "They are stepping-stones to many things." So I took them, hoping desperately that I would discover where it was that I wanted to go. But, you see, I was really quite lost. I didn't know what I wanted to do. I didn't have a goal. I didn't know who I was. During my second year at law school in Toronto,

I became a Christian. Let me explain that. Like many of you I went through the Sunday school bit and joined the church, but it was all pretty meaningless. It was through the steadfastness of a friend that I came to recognize and accept by faith the reality of God's action in time and space in the person of Jesus. I decided that I wanted to put my life under a new management, and so I became a Christian.

The way we speak of such things can sometimes be a little confusing. At Christmas an Israeli friend of my son's was staying with us. One evening he read somewhere that I had said, "When I became a Christian." He said, "I thought you were always a Christian, just as I have always been Jewish." During our conversation I explained to him that for me becoming a Christian was partially being raised in a Christian family and culture, but it also involved, at some point, a conscious decision on my part.

But you see that was not just a religious decision that I made. It was a discovery as to my identity or role. I discovered with the yielding of myself to Christ that I was a child of God, and, as Paul says, "an heir of God." Now that I knew who I was, the obvious question was, "Lord, what do you want me to do to fulfill my new identity? Do you see the difference?

Before I became a Christian, I was trying to find a job or goal, hoping to find myself. I was goal-oriented. Now that I knew who I was, I was trying to find a job or a goal to fulfill me in my new identity as a child of God.

That was the difference between my father and me. But neither of us could see it at that time.

And we see this in so many of our young people these days who are not satisfied to get poured into the system in the hope that they will find themselves. They want to find themselves first and then find a job that is rewarding and satisfying. This is exactly what Marshal McLuhan has been saying. Young people today are not looking for goals, but roles.

All this has a very practical application! It is all very well to be goal-oriented, to describe yourself in terms of goals, the circumstances of your job, your work, your position or responsibility, or your circumstances—which is what most of us are doing—but what happens when you are fired, retired, sick, or the family grows up and no longer needs you, or your wife dies, or your husband runs away, or you are rejected?

If our basic identity depends on any of these things, then we are headed for trouble, because they will all change. Then, like my father—who up until his death had a very real sense of being lost, because he didn't know who he was—we will feel insignificant and worthless. This is a terrible experience, and it isn't confined just to old age.

Let me tell you about three people I know, for whom change was very traumatic.

One is a young man of thirty-six. He dropped in one day to tell me that he had lost his job during the summer. He is married with three small children. He has no special skills, and he is finding it tough to get another job. The constant rejection by potential employers is making him depressed and discouraged, and he is asking some very serious questions. "Who am I?" "Am I really worth anything?" "What have I been doing all my life?" He is not a religious man at all, but he is asking some deeply theological questions.

Now the worst thing that could happen to this fellow would be for him to find another job before he gets some answers to the questions he has been asking, otherwise these important questions will be buried in the new job.

But you see he is a goal-oriented man. His whole identity has been wrapped up in his job and the life-style he has been living is a result of that job. Suddenly his circumstances changed, and he lost not only a job, but also his identity.

Let me tell you about Betty, a friend of mine. When she was in college twenty-five years ago, she was very much in love. But then the man she loved changed his mind and dropped her. The effect of that lost love was shattering, and it really made her feel as if she weren't worth very much. You see, her identity was so wrapped up in her boyfriend's assessment of her that when he said "Get lost," she not only lost her boyfriend, but she lost her sense of self-worth.

Rose is a friend I met at the hospital. She is eighty-eight, bedridden, hard of hearing, and going blind. Rose is lonely and she hurts. But she is a delightful person.

When she was eighteen, she left home and married. Her husband died under tragic circumstances when he was only forty-five. Then her only daughter died at the age of twenty-eight. She has been alone ever since. While she was in a home for the aged in Toronto, she never received a personal visit from anyone in the five years that she was there. Well, as a result of her sickness and the loss of her family, Rose really doesn't think she is very important. She doesn't know who she is any more. She is wishing that she could die.

Dr. William Glasser, the California psychiatrist, says that the greatest problem facing people today, and especially the elderly, is that they don't know who they are.

This sense of lostness happens not just to individuals, but to groups as well, including congregations. When I was the pastor of St. Peter's church in Sudbury, the building was burned to the ground, and six months later I left. Without the building and the minister, many of the people wondered who they were. It was an identity crisis.

Those in the congregation who were goal-oriented, those who found their identity in the church through programs, plans, goals, and through the office of the minister were in trouble. Those who were role-oriented and knew themselves to be the Body of Christ, whose job it is to tell the world about the goodness of God, were confident and assured about the future.

When I read about the early disciples, I have a strong feeling that they knew *who* they were, because they knew *whose* they were. They knew to whom they belonged, in the midst of change.

When Peter was preaching about Jesus and asking the people to repent and be baptized, he wasn't being religious, he was inviting them to discover their real identity. He wanted them to discover an identity that would not change with circumstances or time.

When Peter and John were arrested and abused for their preaching, they still knew who they were. Their identity did not depend on what the world thought or on their circumstances. Their identity was determined by their relationship with Jesus Christ.

It is only when we see our identity and value in relationship to Jesus, who never changes, that we can confidently say each one of us, you and I are important. We say it not because of what we have done or because of who we are, but because of who God is. He is our firm, unchanging foundation. He is the one who loved us so much

27

that he gave his only son. That is John 3:16, and it is a verse about our identity.

Paul put it this way: "In human experience it is a rare thing for one man to give his life for another, even if the latter be a good man, though there have been a few who have had the courage to do it. Yet the proof of God's amazing love is this, that it was while we were yet sinners that Christ died for us" (Romans 5:7-8, Phillips).

Peter said, "You are a 'chosen generation; his 'royal priesthood', his 'holy nation', his 'peculiar people' " (I Peter 2:9, Phillips).

Now these are not only theological statements concerning God, they are identity statements about you and about me. They are the most important statements that were ever made about us. They are statements about the love of God for us. They provide the solid foundation upon which we dare to risk change.

Everything else in the world can deny our importance, our value, and our self-worth. It can happen because of old age, sickness, scandal, sin, poverty, youthfulness, or failing in human relations. But, in the eyes of God, we are so important—each one of us—that Christ died for us. And that never changes.

Herb Bark caught the significance of this on the cover of a Faith at Work magazine. He wrote:

"Believe it,
You are a real find, a joy in someone's heart.
You are a jewel, unique, and priceless.
I don't care how you feel,
Believe it!
God don't make no junk."

So for me the first step to rejoicing and risking change is to affirm who I am and whose I am, and to claim an identity that never changes despite the ups and downs of my life. As I am writing this I am rejoicing because my father before he died, wrote me a letter in which he said:

I seem to be doing a lot of thinking about death. I don't know what prompts it, other than I have passed into my eighties, and it won't last much longer. I watched the Billy Graham show on TV the other night, and I wonder about those people who come to the mike and testify how Christ came into their hearts. I do not know how to do it, and I would like to know.

I wrote to him and told him what I could. When he did what I suggested and invited Jesus to come into his life, Jesus did, because he promised that he would. But what is equally important is that my father, after eighty years of trying to find his identity in terms of his job and circumstances and family, had now found his real identity. He no longer had to describe himself in terms of a job or circumstances that have passed away. He could say with confidence, "I know who I am, I am Ray MacDougall, child of God." And nothing in this world or the next can change that fact.

The Neglected Part

I very often hear people say that there should be more love, joy, enthusiasm, and excitement in the church. Without wishing to give simplistic answers or to undermine the power of the Holy Spirit, I would like to suggest that part of the problem is that we Christians need to learn some facts about our feelings, which we have neglected and avoided for so long. For example:

What we repress as human beings, we become. If you are one who has pushed down the anger in your life over a period of years, it will reveal itself in one way or another.

We cannot be selective about the feelings we repress. If we Christians are going to repress our anger, our hostility, our fears, our resentments, or our doubts, as well as our good feelings about ourselves, we will also find that we've put the lid on our love, compassion, enthusiasm, and joy.

Repression robs us of a great deal of inner energy and drive.

Living in relationship—which is what Christianity is all about—means expressing our true feelings, and so we need to learn how to achieve some measure of wholeness in this area of our lives.

Some people are afraid that acknowledging certain feelings may lead to undesirable actions and behavior, and I must confess that I get nervous in this area too. As Christians we need to be responsible about our feelings.

However, it is not only in the area of feelings that there is danger of irresponsible action. Some Christians are irresponsible in their thinking and actions because they are literalistic, and ignore the context in which the words are spoken. Last year in New Brunswick, I observed a church group offering cold glasses of water to people at a summer fair. No doubt they were being obedient to Jesus' words in Matthew 25. However, the next day it was cold and rainy and wet, but there they were still offering people cold glasses of water. Other Christians are irresponsible in the care of their bodies. So feelings and emotions are just one other area of my life in which there is change, and I want to rejoice.

Recently on a flight to western Canada, somewhere between Winnipeg and Edmonton, I spoke to the woman next to me. She was a supervisor for an insurance company on her way to Edmonton to hire new staff. As we talked, she began to tell me about the different qualities in the branch managers she had met. I asked her if her company believed in woman managers, and if she was likely to become one. The funny thing is that I don't remember her answer. What I do recall is that she began to tell me of the desirability of male managers, because men were more rational and less emotional than women and hence better managers. I suggested that it was not a case of men being less feeling or less emotional as persons, but that culturally boys and men were programmed to believe that it was more masculine to be unemotional, aggressive, unfeeling, and tough. She was not buying my point of view. She really believed the cultural stereotype of what it means to be a man, and that emotions and feelings were not a part of it.

This woman's stereotyped view is the very thing that Sidney Jourrard writes about in his book, *The Transparent Self.* Jourrard points out that this cultural shaping of masculinity results in all sorts of damage to the man's person, his health, and, in some measure at least, accounts for the fact that men die earlier than women.

During the past five years I have begun to discover the reality of feelings. They have probably been the most painful five years of my life because a lot of my past feelings and emotions were so jammed down and repressed that getting in touch with, recognizing and claiming them, has been painful. I don't think that this has made me less masculine. I am sure that it has made me a more sensitive human being, and for that I am rejoicing.

One thing needs to be made clear. When I am talking about feelings and emotions, I am talking about something that I believe is normal, healthy, and God-given. I am not talking about emotionalism, which for me is a neurotic response to life. Neither am I talking about something that is in opposition to reason or rationality. Emotions and feelings are a part of what makes me whole. They are a means to deeper involvement with one's inner self and with others. But they are scary and risky! They make one vulnerable! And in the eyes of some, they make one weak.

I have always been a reasonably feeling person. That is, I feel for others. Maybe a more honest comment would be that I have been one who tries to please others, to make them feel good, and thereby to make them accept me. Then I feel O.K. But I have not been one to express what I have really been feeling because somewhere I got the idea that right relationships, especially with others, depended on accommodation rather than honest confrontation.

A few weeks ago my wife decided to tell me something about our relationship that she felt I ought to know. It wasn't anything big, but after she had shared it with me, I realized how deeply I had been programmed to believe that right relationships are ones that are calm, peaceful, quiet, agreeable, and nonconfronting. So when Isobel confronted me, what I really heard and felt was rejection and "I don't love you." It was only after she said, "Hey, I still love you," that I began to believe and feel that sharing feelings was O.K. and a part of right relationships.

But you see what happens. I'm not only threatened and frightened when someone else is telling me how they are feeling, but I am not comfortable saying how I really feel for fear of rejection and ridicule. I suspect that the reason many men don't want to get in touch with their real feelings and emotions and to report on them, is because of the fear of what will happen. It is not that it is not human or masculine to feel, but it's frightening and risky and often makes us vulnerable.

For the first twenty-five years of my life, wholeness was on two levels—cerebral and physical. The mind should be developed and prepared, in order to get a job, in order to earn money, so that one could get married and raise a family. Keeping in shape physically has always seemed to me to be an ingredient for personal wholeness. Then when I was twenty-five, I discovered another dimension of wholeness, namely, the spiritual. My sense of wholeness reached a new plateau. Putting my life under the management of Jesus Christ brought a sense of inner cohesiveness. And most recently this new dimension of emotions and feelings has been added; it's exciting, it's liberating, and it's painful—but it's very real.

What I've had to learn is that it is O.K. to feel. That, for me, represents a big change. I do have feelings; they are a part of my humanity. Loving as Jesus told us to love is easier when my feelings are not hidden, but are recognized and acknowledged. The church has often been afraid of feelings, but Jesus wasn't, nor was St. Paul.

Jesus felt anger (Matthew 21:12-13). He knew disappointment (Matthew 14:29-30). He experienced grief (John 11:33; Luke 19:41). Jesus knew compassion (Luke 4:38-39; 5:12-13). and he certainly loved (John 14:31; 15:9).

Paul spoke of the reality of anger in Ephesians 4:26, but he said to be responsible about it. He knew disappointment when the Corinthians kicked over the traces. He experienced despair (II Corinthians 1:8, 9); he loved his friends, he was thankful, he was tender, he yearned for them. I don't know why I never really noticed before that honest feelings and emotions were a part of the lives of Jesus and Paul. I guess I was just too busy "head-tripping," and trying to put it all together intellectually. That's O.K., but it is not the whole story.

All this has reminded me that, in some measure at least, I've often missed the mark when dealing with my congregations at the times of death.

I am sure that I was caring and supportive to many in my congregations during bereavement. But I can also remember thinking that if they would really listen to my funeral message about the love of God and the hope we Christians have in the resurrection, they wouldn't "carry on" so. That is, they would be transformed. They would be excited that we have, in the face of death, a message of hope. They would rejoice that they could entrust a loved one to such a God. In plain words, the Christians' hope at death should, I thought, outweigh and overcome the feelings of grief, sadness and despair.

We do have a great hope in Christ at death. Yet I am now convinced that I should also have *assured* those in mourning that it was appropriate and natural and acceptable to express their feelings of grief and uncertainty. There is a part of me today that cringes a little because there is a sense in which my "all is well and victorious,"

my theologically oriented sermons, were helping bury the emotions of the bereaved. If it is
true, that living is being in touch with and
acknowledging one's feelings, then I really was
burying the emotions of the bereaved, as well as
burying the deceased. If I could do it all over
again I would assure those left behind that their
feelings are entirely appropriate, believing that
with that sort of assurance, they could better
hear the message of hope and grace.

How then do we get in touch with our
God-given feelings? Let me make a few sugges-
tions. Ask yourself when you last had a strong
feeling and what it was you felt.

Isobel and I drive from Hamilton to Beamsville
each Monday morning to play tennis. It's about a
thirty-minute drive. Recently she's been reading
a book at the back of which there is a word-list
exercise to help you get in touch with your
feelings. Isobel reads the words, and then we
share with each other whether we have felt the
feeling suggested by the word or not, and
whether or not we reported our feelings to
others. That exercise certainly helps me to
realize that I have feelings, and to get in touch

with them. I need to add that I don't always feel comfortable with what I discover.

A second way is to ask your friends, your spouse, or your children what feelings they are picking up from you. That's a little scary because you begin to discover how perceptive people really are.

Finally, ask God to free you up. He will. When we begin to get in touch with the reality of our own feelings we will not only begin to rejoice in this new area of our being, but we will begin to be more sensitive to others. Then we can enable them to enter into life more effectively.

Bondage from the Past

Recently I was a "programmed patient" at McMaster University Medical Center in Hamilton, Ontario. What happens is that they take ordinary neurotics like me and program them with real case histories for testing medical students and others. So far I have had a "gastric ulcer" and a "multiple sclerosis" patient.

One day the director of one of the training programs asked me to go "underground" and visit five young doctors who had graduated and were training for their Family Practice Specialty Certificate in various clinics around the city of

Hamilton. These doctors had agreed to be part of the program, but they did not know they might get a "programmed patient." After a few hours of rehearsing I made my first visit. Each doctor was to be visited twice. On the first call I would present my physical symptoms. The doctor would examine me. The supervising physician and nurses would be watching through a one-way window and listening through a micro-phone. I would then take the requisitions for tests which the doctor had ordered to the director of the program, who in turn would arrange to have fake results (which said that I was O.K.) sent back to the doctor before my next appointment. On the second call the doctor, if he was on the ball, would begin to zero in and discover that my real problem was "situational anxiety" caused by my job and my family situation. Well, it was all for the cause of medicine and it was fun. It was also "pretend."

However, I am discovering that a lot of us Christians were "programmed for real" as children, and the programming has caused us a lot of bondage and pain.

For the past three years with Faith at Work in Canada, I have traveled across the country telling people that the kingdom of God is the kingdom of right relationships. A right relationship with God, the world, others, and oneself.

If that is so, then the important question is What is a right relationship? My answer has been a beautiful one that I've taken from Karl Olsson, formerly with Faith at Work (U.S.A.). This is what he says, "A right relationship is *not* a perfect relationship, but in the midst of risk and pain, it is growing, loving, open, honest, and confronting." That sounded so neat and I really believed it in my head.

However, over the past six months I have been getting some signals that my stomach really does not believe it. Every time I would get into a confronting situation, the butterflies in my stomach told me that a right relationship does not fit Karl Olsson's definition at all, but rather it is a relationship which is smooth and peaceful and quiet and polite and nice. The old definition has been so strong that when I get into a confronting situation, I begin to be a sixteen-year-old boy trying to please again.

But it has been at home where the signals have been the strongest. Isobel and I have had more hassles in the past year than in the previous twenty-four years of our marriage. I really hate them. I have said I'm sorry more darn times just to clear up the situation, when saying that was very inappropriate.

Well, a few days ago Isobel took one of our children shopping. I warned her that it probably would end up in a hassle, because just as my son Paul and I have our sticky moments, so Isobel has her difficult moments with Jane. But Isobel said "No, it's O.K. I know what is wanted, and it will be all right."

When they returned from shopping, Isobel's first words were, "Never again . . . " Well, I tried to respond in an appropriate way, but everything I said Isobel heard as condemnation. Very soon there wasn't just one hassle in the MacDougall household, there were two. And I knew that Isobel was the cause of the problem.

The next evening when we were talking about the situation, suddenly the lights went on for me. I began to see what was going on in terms of my personal relationships. I was in bondage to the dictum that a right relationship is one that is smooth and polite and nice and peaceful. It was still very much in control of my life.

When I refer to a dictum I mean a maxim that

44

gets laid on us as children either by our preacher, our parents, the community, or by ourselves. It is called a dictum because it continues to control our lives as adults. Some simple dicta that control adult lives are these: Men don't cry. Christians never get angry. Sex is dirty. When we become aware of a dictum in our lives we can either reject it and adopt a new guiding principle or accept it as being good. It is the conscious dealing with a dictum that begins the process of change.

Well, because this dictum that a right relationship is smooth and peaceful was so in control of my life, I had usually handled conflict with Isobel by going silent, sucking my thumb, or eventually saying I'm sorry—whether I was or not.

Of course, by doing that I was not only preventing a healthy reconciliation, I was also cutting her off by withdrawing myself. And by withdrawing myself I was withdrawing my love and isolating her.

Now there have been times when I have shared something of myself with Isobel, and those have been the times when we have felt closest to each other. I *now* see that sharing myself, my needs, my loneliness, and my hurts is really an act of affirmation and love for her. That's why she feels so good about it. I felt better myself, of course, as one who had been able to unload his burdens. Somehow, I never realized before that sharing myself is an act of affirmation of the *other person.*

Dr. Sidney Jourrard has a wonderful chapter in *The Transparent Self* entitled "The Lethal Aspects of the Male Role." It's a marvelous chapter on why men die younger than women. Jourrard feels that it's a man's lack of openness and transparency and vulnerability about himself that adds to the stresses and strains of life and finally to an earlier death. And so Jourrard, for very pragmatic and practical reasons, is urging men to be more open and to risk sharing their feelings, because it could add years to their lives.

But openness in a Christian context, I am discovering, is not just a self-help act done in order to live longer. It's really an act of giving oneself to another. It's an act of love. It's an act of trust and affirmation. And, of course, it is risky. It is dying to self, because it does make you vulnerable. Maybe that is what Jesus meant when he talked about the seed dying in order to live and to bear fruit.

I am beginning to see that that is what the Incarnation was all about. It was an act of self-giving by God. "For God so loved the world that He gave . . . " It was an act of affirmation of us by God. That is what the angel was saying to the shepherds: "Be not afraid; for behold I bring you good news of a great joy which shall be to all people; for to you is born this day in the City of David a Saviour who is Christ the Lord." The angel was announcing God's act of self-giving and affirmation of us, which resulted in risk and pain and death and resurrection. It was an act in which God made himself very vulnerable. And that I believe is what Jesus is inviting us to do.

So I'm beginning to put my head and my stomach together. I'm beginning to understand that my openness about my feelings, while risky, is really an act of saying, "I love you very much because I'm willing to risk giving myself to you."

That is what God is saying to us in Jesus Christ. "I love you so much that I am willing to risk myself with you. You may accept me or you may reject me." That is exactly what John reports.

"He came to his own home and his own people received him not. But to all who received him and believed in his name, he gave the power to become children of God" (1:11-12). It was a risk that God took, but one which his love for us demanded that he take. John puts it so beautifully, "And the Word became flesh and dwelt among us, full of grace and truth (1:14)."

When Isobel and I were talking, I realized that I had been approaching all my personal relationships with this dictum in control: A right relationship is one which is smooth and even and peaceful and quiet and polite.

I was programmed! I was in bondage! And so you see what happens. When Isobel tells me of her hassle with one of the children, my programmed view of right relationships, is really dictating my response, and so what Isobel hears, *no matter what words I use,* is "You're wrong. You could have done better. You should not feel that way. Why don't you smarten up?" And, of course, that just leads to another hassle between us.

It all sounds so incredible because I was so sure that Isobel was the one who was at fault and who needed to shape up. It never occurred to me that I was adding to the problem.

The way I had been handling personal relationships received some objective confirmation at a conference recently. On the first day we completed a test based on our own assessment of our leadership. The results showed me that in the most productive circumstances, I tend to be a controlling, adaptive kind of person. Translated, that means that I am controlling, self-confident, competitive, risk-taking, flexible, and enthusiastic. In less productive situations, where there is conflict, I still tend to be controlling, but in a manner that is domineering, impulsive, and impatient. My adaptiveness tends to become self-denying, passive, and easily influenced. It's getting very close to compromise.

Well, all of that seemed to confirm my suspicions that in stressful situations with certain people, particularly those my own age or older, I tend to relate as a child rather than as an adult. Unintentionally, I become the young person trying to please. It's another manifestation of the dictum "measure up" that has controlled my life for so long. My past is still shaping my present.

49

I am really feeling these days that the Lord is calling me to die to that programmed view about what is a right relationship. I must change, or continue living in bondage. Like Lazarus I feel the Lord saying, "Bruce, come forth to a new concept of right relationships. It is risky and a little frightening. But it's my way and I will be with you, and there will be those in the Body of Christ as well as those not in the body who will support you and help unbind you."

And I want to come out, but I'm frightened of rejection and of being vulnerable.

The important lesson for me is not to determine who in my life programmed me in this way so that I can establish blame, rather it is to discover that in the area of relationships, the grace of God has not really been controlling my behavior as I thought. I can choose to live no longer under the dictum of smooth and pleasant and nice and polite relationships. I want and need a fresh beginning. I want to change by consciously claiming the model of Jesus, so neatly phrased by Karl Olsson—that in the midst of risk and pain a right relationship is growing, loving, open, honest, and confronting. That's the only way that I can enter into adult-to-adult relationships with others as I believe God wants me to do. By the power of the Holy Spirit and the supporting care of my brothers and sisters in Christ I believe that it can be done.

My New Friend

I didn't know how "Greek" I was in my thinking about my body until I read about Snoopy in "Peanuts." It was the day after New Year's, and Snoopy was lying on top of his doghouse saying "Why doesn't someone shoot me and get it over with?" It had been a great party, but Snoopy had eaten more than he should, danced too long, and had a little too much to drink. He was very conscious that his feet were complaining, his stomach was upset, and his head was aching. He was finding it all a bit much, and so he said, "The next time I go somewhere, I'll leave you all at home."

Well that was me! For the first twenty-five years of my life my body was a burden too. I had lung cancer, disc problems, arthritis, colitis, ulcers, and several coronaries. At least I thought I did.

What was happening was that my body was just reflecting my sense of anxiety, my lostness, and my inordinate self-concern. My body really was my enemy. It worried me, it hurt me, it restricted me, it was a drag. If there had been any way of getting rid of it and living, I would have done it. Like Snoopy I would have left it at home.

I would like to suggest to you that most of us Christians need a broader concept of wholeness. In the past, says Karl Olsson, the church has tended to localize salvation in one or two areas.

For example, the church has said that to be whole one must be doctrinally correct. Or it has said that confessing one's sins will make one whole. Or, making a decision for Jesus Christ is what is required for wholeness. The trouble is that we all know people who are orthodox in their belief, but who are not whole. We know people who are open about their sins, yet remain unhealed. And we know people who have made a decision for Christ and still need to be healed.

Christian wholeness is larger than any one, or even all three of these areas of life. There are other parts to our wholeness such as our emotions, our personal relationships, our caring outreach to others, and our own bodies. And each of these areas of life is essential to our salvation, our wholeness. When we neglect any one of these areas it affects all the rest.

One area of wholeness that is often neglected by Christians is the area of physical wholeness. I'd like to share with you some things that I have discovered about my new friend, my body. And it has been an experience in which I rejoice.

St. John's Gospel says, "In the beginning was the Word . . . and the Word was made flesh" (1:1,14). The writer of that Gospel is a real communicator. He has a fantastic message to proclaim, and he knows that at least two different types of people will be reading his message—Jews and Gentiles. So he has to be very careful about the words that he chooses. To get across his main idea he selects the Greek word *Logos,* which means "the word." He knows that his Jewish and Greek readers will bring their own meaning to that word. *Logos*, says William Temple in his writings, "could mean to the Jews the Word of the Lord by which the heavens were made and which came to the prophets, or to the Greeks, it could mean the rational principle which gives unity and significance to all existing things." John uses the word *Logos* because he is seeking a common ground between the Jews and the Greeks. There would be no use telling the Gentiles that the Messiah had come, because they were not expecting a messiah. And so John chooses a word which represents for both the Jew and the Greek the "ruling fact of the universe," and he represents that fact as a self-expression of God. So when John uses the word *Logos* the Jews would remember that by the Word of the Lord were the heavens made, and the Greeks would think of the rational principle behind all things. But both would agree that this *Logos* is the starting point of all things.

Now that he has his audience where he wants them, John says that this *Logos* has become flesh and dwelt among us and that is the good news.

The good news of Christianity is not that God loves us or that God is a loving God, but rather that God so loved the world that he acted. God has acted in a particular time in space and history.

The Word became flesh! That's the good news.

I have always tended to think of these passages about the birth of Jesus in theological terms, which of course was appropriate, but here I want to shift our focus, not away from the fact of God's action in history, but to the *means* of God's action by which he presented himself to us.

Luke says, "You will find a babe wrapped in swaddling clothes." John says, "The Word was made flesh and dwelt among us." What they are saying to us, according to Archbishop William Temple, is that the Word did not merely reside within a human being, but that absolute identity is asserted. The Word is Jesus, and Jesus is the Word. These gospel writers are telling us that in Jesus the *flesh* is a completely responsive vehicle of the Spirit. The whole of Jesus, his flesh included, is the Word, the self-utterance of God.

Now that is important to me because so often the word "flesh" carries with it the connotation of frailty, weakness, and sin. But John is telling us that the flesh is *not incompatible* with being in the Spirit.The body is not the anthithesis of the spirit. The body is the means by which God presented himself to us.

Of course we are all conscious that by

definition the flesh is the earthly part of us. It has its lusts and desires. If a person concentrates on these he may properly be said to have set his mind on "the things of the flesh." And the "mind of the flesh" is death. Paul makes it clear that a man whose mind is limited by the flesh is opposed to God. So the flesh can be directed to earthly pursuits and not to serving God. *But* that is equally true of our minds and our relationships. They too can be directed to the things of the flesh and be opposed to God.

The exciting thing for me is that the gospel writers are making it clear that our bodies are not incompatible with "being in the Lord," because the Lord himself chose the flesh as a means to present himself to us.

I suspect that most of us Christians, in our view of the body, are like Snoopy, more Greek than biblical. The Greeks saw the soul as being imprisoned in the body with death as the means of releasing the soul. The biblical view sees the body as a whole with emphasis on the resurrection. The Greeks viewed the body as alien, or the enemy of the soul.

After I became a Christian, that commitment to God, even though it was little understood, brought a new unity and cohesiveness to my whole being. That conversion experience, plus some straight talk to me from a doctor friend, brought me a new wholeness and freedom that was almost immediately reflected in new bodily health.

Now I am not saying that as a Christian I have no physical problems or needs, but *now* when my body hurts, I listen to this friend, because my body, like my conscience is a friend. And sometimes it tries to get my attention through aches and pains (just like Snoopy's).

Well, if our bodies are our friends then I believe that there are some inferences that we can draw from the biblical view of our bodies. We should be aware of our bodies, and love and cherish them. We must communicate with them. After a tennis match this summer I was very conscious of how well my body (my feet, legs, arms, etc.) had served me, and as I stood in the shower, I said, "Thank you body. Thank you feet, etc." And it made sense.

Our bodies are aware of us, too. They care for us and try to communicate with us by mute signals such as "What are you trying to do to me?" Or "What are you trying to do to yourself?"

These signals can be a pain, some form of illness, poor posture, or unwanted weight.

If it is true that my body is a responsive vehicle of God's presence and a friend to be cherished and cared for, that gives me good reason to celebrate my body, to accept it, and to rejoice in it.

Last Sunday in church five young women danced during the service and interpreted the Twenty-third Psalm. Their bodies were not only beautiful, but they used them to present and interpret God's love to us. Now we can't all be dancers. Some of us don't have the shape or the coordination. But because God has come to us in the flesh, that has given me a new attitude and love and acceptance of the body. I'm discovering that it is an effective means of showing my love, and sometimes God's love as I understand it, to others. Just think of how empty and frustrating love would be if we didn't have bodies to be touched and hugged and cared for. I am rejoicing for the fresh discovery that the good news is not confined to my head or my feelings or my emotions or my relationships, but that it also includes my body.

Mortality Is Scary

Last month my son Paul and I went to Hamilton Place to listen to a band playing the music of Jelly Roll Morton. Morton, I am told, may have been the inventor of New Orleans jazz. The band playing his music was very exciting. As I listened, every tissue, cell, and muscle in my being was alive. My fifteen-year-old son, Paul,was a little embarrassed by my feet tapping to the music.

It is funny that in the middle of the concert I should think of First Corinthians 15 where Paul (not my son) talks about the resurrection life. I wondered to my self if there would be piano players like Jelly Roll Morton in the resurrection. Would I be able to hear him? If so, would there be pianos, too? Well I hope so!

When I got home I reread First Corinthians 15, but Paul does not make it clear, does he? Someone had asked Paul what kind of bodies we would have in the resurrection life. Paul responded that they were pretty dumb to ask the question. He told them that they would have bodies in the resurrection life which would be appropriate to the occasion. But nobody asked Paul if in the resurrection life we would be able to do things we have done here on earth, or listen to people like Jelly Roll Morton, or whether we would be able to do things we have not been able to do here in this life. I wish they had asked. Paul does not say and I don't know.

There was a time when just "knowing" that there would be a resurrection life was enough. That was when I was young enough to think that I was going to live forever, or at least death by old age seemed so far away that it was of no concern. But now I am in a process of change. I'm in my fifties, and I am getting hints that I am not immortal. I notice myself reacting to that. For instance, I find myself trying very hard to prove that I've still got lots of life. Our vacation cottage is located in a very tennis-oriented community. There is just something about that game that really turns me on. It brings out all of my competitive nature. During the summer I managed to get in about two or three hours of tennis a day. Once a week the club sponsors a round robin tournament. Couples are rather arbitrarily put together, and there is a play-off until one couple wins. I had always lost in the first match and ended up in the consolation round.

One evening in August, I was paired with a sixteen-year-old girl who had pigtails and horn-rimmed glasses. My first reaction was "Uh-oh, here we go again." And then she hit the ball. It flew across the net as if it had been shot out of a cannon. Wow! She was terrific. As a result I played a mile over my head, and four hours later we had won. I could hardly believe it. For the next two days I could hardly walk, but it was a great feeling. I never had won anything before in athletics, and to win at my age was really a thrill.

But I have also been getting some outside objective hints that I'm in a change process, or perhaps I should say decay. As a matter of fact I've had three hints concerning my mortality in the recent past. First, while being examined for a hernia operation an intern said, "Man, I wish I were in your shape." That made me really feel good until he added, "When I get to be your age." Suddenly I felt older. I made some flip comment, but it really was a cover-up.

Secondly, Isobel and I are buying a house. I phoned an insurance agent about some mortgage insurance to cover the amount of the mortgage. The agent gave me some quotations based on a twenty-year term. When I asked for a quote on a twenty-five year term because that was the term of the mortgage, the agent replied, "I am sorry Mr. MacDougall, but we can't give *you* twenty-five years at your age." I made some sort of smart comment, but down deep I really wanted to say, "Hey, my father lived to eighty-four, my mother is eighty-two, I'm very active, and don't you read the United Church Observer obituary column? We clergy all live to a ripe old age." But I didn't.

While in Florida recently, Isobel and I were lying on the beach. The sky was blue, the sun was hot, and I was trying to get a tan and at the same time memorize the second chapter of

Paul's Letter to the Philippians. I soon discovered that there were some real distractions to
memorizing scripture. Those Swedish bathing
suits that the girls were wearing reminded me
very forcibly that though I still had an eye for a
beautiful girl, they were not eyeing me. I was just
another middle-aged man who, statistically
speaking, only had twenty more years.

I frankly need a word of comfort and encouragement in my awareness of change and aging.

In Faith at Work we spend a lot of time talking
about the now and the present and the importance of relationships and the open life-style.
And all that is very important. And when we do
that, we are really saying that we are the media
for the message of hope and freedom to the
world. That is scripturally true, too. Paul says to
his friends at Philippi, "Shine as lights in the
world" (2:15). He tells his Corinthian friends,
"You yourselves are our letter of recommenda-
tion written on your hearts, to be known and
loved by all men" (II Corinthians 3:2).

But sometimes the message itself is the
medium for hope and freedom and confidence in
our hearts. And that has certainly been true for
me now in my middle-age anxiety.

MORTALITY IS SCARY

It happened in church on Sunday. We sang that exciting new song "He Arose." It was very reassuring and made me feel good. Then a young high school girl read the scripture lesson from Romans, which ends with Paul saying, "For I am sure that neither death, nor life, nor angels, nor principalities, nor things present, nor things to come, nor powers, nor height, nor depth, nor anything else in all creation, will be able to separate us from the love of God in Christ Jesus our Lord" (8:38). That in turn made me think of how Paul reminds us that "if we live, we live unto the Lord, and if we die, we die unto the Lord; so then, whether we live or whether we die, we are the Lord's. For to this end Christ died and lived again that he might be Lord both of the living and of the dead" (Romans 14:8-9).

But perhaps my greatest encouragement about death came through a dear friend, Ruth. For a year-and-a-half she has been struggling with cancer. Ruth was a very vivacious, live-in-the-present person who made you feel good just being with her. During her illness it was no different. She was able to be so "up front" about it all in terms of her feelings of faith, fear, anxiety, hope, anger, and acceptance that she enabled many of us to face the reality of our own deaths in a more positive way. It is funny how some people who are seriously ill get increasingly more isolated as death approaches, but not Ruth. In fact, the contrary was true. When she finally had to be admitted to the hospital for the last time, someone from the congregation was with her twenty-four hours a day. Ruth was no paper saint, but she really did know something about living totally in the now even as she faced death. And that was an encouragement to me.

I don't know whether there are going to be any Jelly Roll Mortons or pianos in the resurrection life or not. I don't know whether I'll get to be seventy-five, but I do know that I am getting older. I am coming to grips with the reality of my death. I am in an aging process for which the gospel is still good news. Jesus Christ was Lord when I was twenty-five. He is still Lord. In that belief, by faith, I more confidently face the reality of my mortality. And that is a change!

The Treasure Is in the People

When I was a layman in a large church in Ottawa, the minister was really a cut above the rest of us.

He was the leader! He was the one to whom we looked for inspiration and guidance and wise counsel. It was his preaching that brought the large crowds to the morning and evening services.

When I became a clergyman I accepted that role quite readily. After all, what layman had taken systematic theology or homiletics or New or Old Testament? However, when I got to my

67

first pastoral charge there were lay men and women to share the responsibility of spiritual nurture with me. I spent a great deal of time preparing them to be responsible leaders. I wrote pamphlets for them on baptism, confirmation, eldership, and death. We ran school for elders and stewards. There were those who were really interested in trying to help and who wanted to be what I wanted them to be, but for the most part they were reluctant and frustrated. There was no way that we could reenact First Corinthians 12. If there were gifts in the church, I was sure that, at least in my congregation, I possessed most of them.

The first step in my reeducation and change began one weekend in the fall of my second year at St. Peter's in Sudbury, Ontario. Someone invited me to attend the Elgin House Fellowship which had been started by Quinton Warner. Quint was a friend of Sam Shoemaker, and he, with some friends, had conceived of a yearly conference where people could come and share what the Lord was doing in their lives. When I arrived that fall, I heard lay people and the clergy from a variety of denominations openly sharing what was happening in their lives, and how they understood God to have met them in those circumstances. The reality of their faith was unmistakable and exciting.

I knew what God had done for my life. Back home I spent each Sunday telling my congregation what he would do for their lives if they would only respond. Somehow what I was doing back home was not working as I thought it should. But here at the Elgin House Fellowship were ordinary men and women sharing out of the reality of their lives, and people were responding as I had never seen before. It was then that I began to see the power and treasure in the laity. Here was a way of communicating the gospel that they had never mentioned at the seminary. By sharing themselves, which was the most precious thing they had to share, these men and women were enabling others to express their needs and hopes and dreams, and to discover the reality of God precisely where they were.

As a result of this new awareness of the lay person's role, we held a Faith at Work Conference at St. Peter's Church. A group of fourteen lay people from Southern Ontario came and shared with the congregation what God was doing in their lives. After the conference, nine small sharing/Bible study groups began. I was not the leader of any of them. Each group had from five to a dozen members. They shared with each other, cared for each other, and prayed for each other.

These groups soon became the places where I could send others who needed fellowship and support. The point is, that these lay people were discovering a new ministry based on openness and sharing and accountability. They were no longer just helping me in my ministry, they were exercising their own ministries, with my blessing and gratitude. They were beginning to discover their gifts. Some had the gift of discernment, others the gift of love, others patience and availability. They were the Body of Christ! Their several gifts were making others whole. I need to be careful that I do not claim too much for these small groups. They were not a panacea for my church or for those who attended. *Sometimes* they functioned beautifully. *Sometimes* they seemed to be falling apart. But throughout it all, they were the Body. They were a foretaste. And these groups gave to those who attended a new kind of confidence in lay ministry that they never had before. The opportunity to use that new confidence in a more public and community way was soon to arise.

One day, about a year and a half after the Faith at Work Conference, I read in a news magazine about a twenty-four-hour telephone ministry in Sidney, Australia, operating under the name LifeLine. The originator of this ministry was Alan Walker of the Sidney Methodist Mission. The article told of trained lay people who manned the several telephones twenty-four hours a day for people in distress. In their first year they received fifteen thousand calls.

It sounded like the kind of ministry we ought to have in Sudbury. After several months of preparation, we held a public meeting to announce our first training program. Of the fifty or so people who enrolled, the majority were members of the small sharing groups of my own church. With their new sense of ministry, they saw LifeLine as a greater opportunity for their care and love to others. Their response was also, to me, a great vindication of the small group approach. Many people have criticized small groups for being too introspective. But as a result of that year and a half of personal growth in the small groups, these people came forward when they saw the opportunities for serving others. They were not only the majority in that first class, but they remained for years as the solid core of those who made the telephone ministry work.

One of the great difficulties in moving from a ministry in small groups to a more public ministry on the telephone is the sense of inadequacy felt by most lay people. I believe this sense of inadequacy has been laid on the laity by the professionals—including the clergy—who have convinced them that unless you have a Ph.D. in psychology or an advanced degree in social work or theology, you really have nothing to offer people in need.

Of course we are past that myth today, but thirteen years ago the LifeLine training program was really a pioneer effort in preparing lay people for useful ministry in the church and for the community at large. We sought to equip our workers through several months of study, during which the best professional leadership in the community came to share what they knew about certain areas of distress.

There is a sense in which that kind of professional input is dangerous. It can either make the workers think that they are quasi-professional, or reinforce their sense of inadequacy because the problems are so complex. Some people fell into the trap of thinking that if they just had enough information and facts about all the problems from the professionals, then they could help the caller. They became our problem-solvers. Others saw the needs of the caller as an opportunity for evangelism. Because this was a ministry and outreach of the church there was a constant tension between just plain listening to people and wanting to use the occasion to read the Bible and pray with them. But through it all the workers learned, they grew, and they did the job.

LifeLine was in the beginning centered in Sudbury. It is now the oldest such volunteer center in North America. Today there are nineteen other centers in the provinces of Ontario and Manitoba operating under the new name of Telecare. They have some eight hundred workers and receive some 58,000 calls per year. Telecare Canada is associated with centers in the United States and nine other countries around the world, involving more than twenty thousand volunteers. Altogether they receive more than two million calls per year. It has truly become a network of compassion around the world.

Bruce Larson in his book *The Relational Revolution* says that anyone with average ability and intellect and sensitivity can risk becoming involved with a fellow human being who is struggling with a personal problem.

Later in the same book Larson says

This is the day of the paraprofessional . . . the day of the layman priest. God has called his church to be a royal priesthood. This means that every believer is a priest, one who mediates strength and grace and healing from God to people. This is the exciting adventure. Each of us can be a resource to another person in the time when he is ready to grow. We can learn how to listen to people deeply, to respect them, to understand them, to empathize, to identify, to be a friend to a friend.

Well, that is what the telephone ministry is all about. Christian lay men and women ministering to the world with the credentials of love and care and affirmation and hope—and the Holy Spirit.

But I believe that there is more than just

"training" involved for the laity to become a priesthood to others and to discover their gifts. The most effective way for lay people to spread the grace of God to others is not by passively receiving lectures from knowledgeable professionals, but chiefly by a personal life-style which is characterized by openness, transparency, vulnerability, and accountability. That is the reason a community of faith is so important for this ministry.

I believe that we must not only minister out of a context of sound theology and professional support but also out of our own humanity. Christians can get their theology and teaching from the church and the seminaries. They can learn sensitivity from those with special skills. They can be informed about the unusual needs of certain hurting people. But I want to suggest that they can only minister to others out of their own humanness as they develop a life-style of openness, and make themselves known to others.

I am sure that is why Jesus spent so much time telling his disciples to love one another. It would be out of a context of loving each other and being loved, of ministering and being ministered unto, of knowing and being known, that they would go out and minister to the world most effectively.

I have noticed that after I have been open and have been known by others and received their ministry that I hear and see and respond to people differently. When I am "theologically hot" I hear people as those who need to be "saved," who need to be changed (my way), and who need to hear my good word. When I am "clinically sharp," I am objective and detached, and I see their problems clearly. When I am "factually aware," I put people in the proper pigeonholes as manipulators or irresponsible, or whatever, and refer them to the appropriate agency.

But when I have been ministered unto by others, because they know me, then I begin to hear and see others as hurting, anxious, rebellious, sinful, frightened, inconsistent men and women just like me, whom Jesus loves with a love beyond my understanding, and he wants to touch them through me and affirm them and draw them close.

So I have another reason to rejoice. I am grateful to those men and women at Elgin House and Telecare who taught me about a width and height and breadth of gifts possessed by ordinary people that I never knew before and without which there is no church. Stan Jones, director of Local Church Ministries of Faith at Work (U.S.A.), has said it best in his expression "The treasure is in the people."

Rejoice Now

Well it happened again! There I was in seat 121 of Hamilton Place listening to the Preservation Hall Jazz Band, and all of a sudden all sorts of scripture went streaking through my head.

Have you ever heard this band? They are something else! The trombonist is eighty-four, the clarinetist is seventy-six, the trumpet player is seventy-two, the drummer is seventy-two, and the piano player is a mere sixty-three. But the music is free and spirited, and I left Hamilton Place with my feet dancing and my heart rejoicing. It was real soul music.

78

REJOICE NOW

The Preservation Hall Band, in spite of the age of its members, doesn't make me think of heaven (though some of them are probably closer than they'd like). Rather, these men make me think of the now. I believe that it was their *now*-living that made them so vital, so in touch with the audience, and so much fun.

On my last birthday I received two books from my children, *Learning to Grow Old* and *How to Stay Young While Growing Older,* and there's lots of good advice in them about making choices and right attitudes and taking vitamin C. But I believe that the Preservation Hall Band has the better answer. *Be in touch with what is going on in your life now,* whether you are twenty or fifty or seventy-five. If you are living where you are *now,* then life will be worthwhile and the juices will flow.

Jesus was really concerned with living now. Just think about that! When Nicodemus came to Jesus looking for some answers, Jesus told him about a new birth and a new spirit. He was really telling Nicodemus how to live in the now. When the rich, young ruler asked Jesus what he could do to have eternal life, Jesus responded by telling him what he could do in order to live now. When

Jesus met the woman at the well, he told her that whoever drank the water that he would give, would never thirst again. He was telling her how to live now. John tells us, in the tenth chapter of his Gospel, that Jesus in speaking to the Pharisees said, "I came that they might have life, and have it more abundantly." He was talking about living to the fullest—now.

Let me just give you one more example. During the Feast of Tabernacles, on the last day of the feast, Jesus stood up and said, "If any one thirsts, let him come to me and drink. He who believes in me, as the scripture has said, 'out of his heart shall flow rivers of living waters' " (John 7:37-38). Isn't that a statement of living now? It surely sounds that way to me.

I don't know about you, but when I read these things about living in the now, I realize I know it in my head, and I find it very exciting stuff, but I also recognize the great distance between my head and my daily life. I seem to always be living in the future. That is where the excitement is . . . in the next event. When I am at a conference in western Canada, I am thinking about the next weekend in Toronto. In Toronto, I'm thinking, "Wouldn't it be nice to be taking a sauna bath somewhere and relaxing." When I get to the sauna, I'm planning the next event, and so it goes. Planning for the future is exciting and demanding. The anticipation is rather exhilarating. The trouble is that living in the future prevents me from being totally present where I am. That detracts from my own enjoyment and deep involvement with others. In fact it sometimes may be a way of avoiding involvement.

The question for me then is how can I change? How can I effectively get hold of the motivation and the power for now, present-tense living?

Maybe there is a clue in the Bible references I used earlier. Each one of these people—Nicodemus, the rich young ruler, and the woman at the well—*had a need.* Even though they didn't voice their need, Jesus spoke to it: the need for a childlike spirit; the need to get rid of those things that were in the way of life; the need to straighten out relationships. And it was at the *point of need* that Jesus spoke the word for now-living.

I think this is true for me. When I share my need with the Lord, and particularly in the presence of another (or other members of his body), or when I recognize in myself a need to which I can admit, it provides an opportunity for putting my head and my life together for some now-living.

The other day I was reading about Zacchaeus. Here was a man who wanted to be in touch with the now. He didn't want to be bound by the past anymore or the oughts or the shoulds that the crowd were trying to lay on him. So he went to see Jesus, and when Jesus said, "Zacchaeus, come down, I want to spend some time with you" (Luke 19:5), he was really saying, "Come with me and learn to live now." And Zacchaeus rushed down from the tree and stepped into a vital now.

Of course, for Zacchaeus the doorway to now-living was opened by Jesus' invitation, but if you remember, Zacchaeus had something to do before he went to dinner. He needed to confess. That was his need. Jesus' invitation shows that we don't need to do anything in order to be affirmed and received by Jesus. But having been affirmed, having experienced the unearned love and care of Jesus, Zacchaeus knew that he could now unload the junk that he had been carrying. Indeed, my guess is that he had been looking for the opportunity, because it was preventing him from living in the now. And it is important to notice that in his confession he did not confess to a failure to live up to the expectations or moral laws of the crowd. That would have been false guilt. (And that's when I get hooked so often—failing to live up to other people's expectations of what a minister should be, or what a parent should be, or a husband.) Zacchaeus confessed to real guilt (cheating people), which I am sure was contrary to his own understanding of right and wrong. He was now free to go to dinner with Jesus and begin the process of living in the now.

Last summer I decided to attend a continuing education course given by George Williams College near Chicago. The course was supposed to be on group process, but instead it turned out to be an eight-day sensitivity course. I had never been to such an event before in a secular context, but I experienced living in the now very intensely. During the eight days, I was on an energy jag like never before. I was up at seven, walked a mile before breakfast, then "processed" in the group till noon. After lunch we played tennis or volley ball and swam till three. Then we did more "processing" till supper. At 7:30 we met and "processed" till about 10:30.

We then went to a nearby restaurant and talked until after midnight. I then walked a mile back to the center and went to bed.

I was totally present to these people until the very last second that I left. In retrospect I have tried to account for the intensity of living during that week. It is important for me to understand because it was the first time in all my travels that *I* did not spoil my time away from home by getting lonely or by emotionally leaving the event three days before it was over.

I became aware of another dictum which had been saying that a husband and father should not have a good time apart from his wife and family. But I had had a marvellous time. When I got home I was able to tell them that while I missed them, I had had a super time. Saying that really felt good!

But why? Well, I can't be absolutely sure, but I believe that in those encounters with Jesus we discussed earlier, a universal law was being expressed. In each case there was a need to which Jesus spoke and which, if responded to, would result in new life in the present.

Although I went to that sensitivity course with no conscious agenda, I soon became aware of some very deep, ambivalent feelings concerning my mother who now lives with us. Because of the openness of the group and the skill of the leader, I was able to get in touch with those feelings, explore them, express them, face them, and own them. It was a tremendous release. It really did feel like a great burden had been lifted, and suddenly there was a surge of energy and zest for life.

Now it was not a church situation. Nobody was talking about Jesus. But maybe this is the general truth about life that applies whether the context is Christian or not, namely, that being confronted with a deeply felt need and dealing with it is the gateway to new, present-tense living.

My guess is that good psychology would say amen to that. In any event it was a welcome change. And I now struggle to appropriate the truth of it to my life. If you are fully living where you are, then life is worthwhile and the juices will flow. So here's to the Preservation Hall Band!

Stop Passing the Buck

I have a feeling that we Christians too quickly and too glibly say that the grace of God or the Holy Spirit in in charge of our lives and our decisions. I confess that I am having difficulty feeling comfortable with people who explain all their decisions or experiences by saying "the Lord led me" or "it was of the Lord." I am discovering that I'm not so sure who or what is running my life and making my decisions until some major or minor crisis hits me. Then I find out, and very often I am surprised.

After I began the Christian life, I had a feeling

that I should be doing something other than the practice of law. I prayed about it, asking God for directions. But I also had lunch for three years on a regular basis with a friend who listened patiently and who I hoped would one day say go into the ministry. He never did, and I finally had to make my own decision. I am sure that the prayer and the luncheons were part of God's process, but I had to decide.

Several years ago I was invited to accept a position in the United States. I couldn't make up my mind. Someone suggested that I take the next step, which was to talk to the American Consul in Toronto. The officer told me that it would probably take two years to get a work permit, and I said to myself, "Thank you Lord, and the U.S. Government, for making my decision." Just as I was about to leave, the consulate employee said that he would double-check his information, and when he returned he said that for clergy the work permit time was only sixty days. The decision was mine again.

The other day my favorite clothier had their annual February sale. I tried on a sports jacket and really liked it, but I felt that I just could not afford it. When I got home I told Isobel about the sale and this terrific $80 jacket for only $39. "Why didn't you buy it?" she asked. The next day I did. But you see what I had done. I had really manipulated Isobel into making my decision, although she didn't know it.

The volitional is another area in my life where I live at two levels. On the one hand I know in my head that I am free and secure in God's acceptance of me. I know that should result in an awareness that I can choose, can commit myself, can arise and walk—that I can decide. But it obviously does not work out that way at the level of feelings and behavior. There are some real blocks to effective decision-making in my life. I keep waiting for God to tell me what to do, either directly or through someone else. I have real trouble with the view that I am in charge, albeit under God.

Just a few weeks ago Isobel and I were on our way to spend a few days in Florida with friends. During the trip, I was offered a job that, for me, would have been the pinnacle of success. It offered unlimited opportunity, time to close out my present responsibilities, generous financial benefits, prestige, status, and the excitement of moving to another country. I told them that I would let them know in a week, because I was sure God would let me know what to do in seven days. Almost immediately I was back to my old tactics. I phoned a real estate agent in the area where the job was located to ask about housing costs. Because we have a large family I was sure the house would cost more than I could handle, based on prices in Toronto and Hamilton, and that would decide the issue. Unfortunately, the prices were well within my salary range, and the decision was mine again. As Isobel and I drove to Florida we made lists of the pros and the cons, and when we arrived in Florida we shared the news with our hosts, hoping, I am sure, that maybe they would say something that would tell me what to do. By the deadline I could not decide. Where was God? He hadn't let me know! One minute I was sure I should accept, the next, that I should not. Finally I phoned and said that I was not free to leave Canada. That was not true! The fact is that I could not decide. The next morning I woke at 5 A.M. convinced that I had just made the greatest mistake of my life. I became aware of an old dictum which my father used to tell me, "If you haven't made it by forty-five, you never will, because they don't want you after that age." When I left law to enter the ministry my father had great difflculty in equating the small suburban church I had in Sudbury with the kingdom of God. That was not "making it" in his eyes. He would have felt O.K. if I had been the minister of Timothy Eaton United Church, which is the largest United Church in Canada. So here I was at fifty-one, and I had just said no to the biggest offer of my life (at least so I thought), and at my age I was sure no one would ever ask me again.

I don't know what "making it" really means, except that it sounds like and feels like being somebody. It also implies recognition and acceptance, and I want and need that very much. I know in my head that in a very real sense a Christian always has these things. It really does not matter where you are or what you are doing, you are somebody. Paul says it very clearly, "We are heirs and joint heirs of God." I know that! But my humanness and my feelings betray my head knowledge, and moments of decision like this just show me how great is the distance between my head and my feelings. I want to "make it."

I was so unhappy about my decision that I phoned back and asked for twenty-four hours more. I remembered a friend close at hand who might, if I talked to him, help me work it through. When I called, he listened very affirmingly. He said that it didn't matter which job I took, but that I should not let them go by default. I needed to decide by faith to go or stay, and then it would be O.K. That way, he said I could not lose. At the end of the conversation I felt my previous decision was right. I could now own it by faith, and I rejoiced.

I have never found decision-making easy, as you now know, for I have been bound by dicta from the past. I have tried to live up to the expectations of other people, and I have been afraid of rejection and making mistakes. All of these have been real blocks to effective decision-making in my life. Despite the blocks and the pain and the distress, there have been some helps. The Christian community has listened and stood by. And I have had an awareness (sometimes in retrospect) of God's presence. There were moments in this most recent experience when I felt like Mary and Martha, "Lord if you had only been here I would not have had to suffer this way." But he was present and did sustain me through the experience, to make my own decision.

I have a lot of friends who seem to have four or five snappy rules for getting God's guidance. It has never worked for me, although I have done all the suggested steps. I had a woman in my congregation in Sudbury, Ontario, who believed that guidance was very easily obtained. All you had to do was pray, check the scriptures to make sure what you were considering was not contrary to God's word, seek the guidance and counsel of Christian friends, make sure it was for service, not self, and somewhere in that process you would come to a decision that was of the Lord. However, when she faced a decision about moving to another university, the guidance didn't come despite her application of the rules. And secretly I rejoiced. She finally had to make the difficult decision herself and own it. And for me that is what decision-making is all about as a Christian. It is not being sure. It is not having a guarantee. It is risky. It could be wrong. But if I make it trusting the Lord to be with me, right or wrong, then it really is O.K. It is not a case of God leaving me if I make the wrong choice. He is the Lord of the living and the dead and of the right decisions and the wrong decisions. So I guess that at the age of fifty-two, I am beginning to take responsibility for my life. I don't want to pass the buck again to friends, or the rules and regulations of another country or a realtor or even God. I want to be responsible for my life under the grace of God, and that is a thing to rejoice about!

Hurrah for Kids

Mark 10:13-16 is the familiar story of the children being brought to Jesus. You will remember that in the story there are three groups of people, plus Jesus. These groups consisted of "they," who I assume are mothers and fathers (because the Greek word for "they" is masculine), the disciples, and the children. We don't know whether they are babies or older children.

When I read this story I tried to get into it by imagining what the feelings of the various people would have been. I think the parents were excited and hopeful because their children might be blessed by this new teacher, were anxious that they might be missed, and were feeling terribly put down and angry when the disciples tried to dismiss them. The disciples were feeling rather protective of Jesus, perhaps because he was tired, and so they found the parents and the children to be annoying. And then, of course, they felt very much misunderstood and rebuked when Jesus did not back them up and said to them, "Let the children come unto me."

It's hard to guess what the children were feeling, but my guess is that they would pick up the vibrations of their parents and therefore experience a wide range of feelings from excitement to bewilderment to anxiety. Jesus clearly was experiencing indignation, compassion, warmth, and disappointment. The disciples thought the children were a nuisance and not very important. Jesus, on the other hand, is affirming the children. He is saying that it is wonderful to be a child because of certain qualities children possess which allow them to receive the gift of the kingdom of God.

The question then is, what are the qualities of children that Jesus speaks of as being essential to the entering into the kingdom of God? Well, there are some obvious qualities, such as trust, openness, weakness, dependency, love, and unworldliness; and Jesus seems to be saying that if we don't possess these qualities it is very difficult to enter into the kingdom of God.

And that is where the story usually ends. That is usually the bottom line, and when it stops there it really hasn't touched me where I am.

So I have been wondering what other words or phrases would be descriptive of childlike qualities, qualities with which I could identify. In other words what kind of person is it that is trusting and loving and open and weak and dependent and unworldly in terms of his or her behavior and actions? How would I recognize such a person?

I am only speculating, but I think Jesus is saying that to be a person who has these childlike qualities you must be a person who is able to . . .

jump for joy,

laugh freely,

cry when you're hurting,

ask for help,

show love when you feel it,

admit when you're afraid and lonely,
clap with excitement,
whistle,
stomp your feet,
be uninhibited and spon-
taneous

Children, by and large, do these things, and Jesus is saying "all right!"

People who are like that are people who have the qualities of children and are therefore able to receive or enter into the kingdom of God. That kind of person is open to the gift of the kingdom. He or she is able to believe in God's love. So Jesus is saying, "Hurrah for kids!" He took them up in his arms and he blessed them.

Now I must be careful. I am not declaring a new kind of legalism which says that if you can laugh, clap, stomp your feet, cry and hug, you are in the kingdom of God. These are simply the qualities that most easily facilitate the accep-tance of and the entering into the kingdom of God. These are qualities which children usually possess. But I need to take them seriously since Jesus said they were important.

The only trouble is that having read the story

about the children, I am not sure that I qualify. I am not a child any more. I am one of your usual inhibited, unspontaneous, waspy adults. So I am wondering whether or not I can get into the kingdom of God, and if I'm in trouble, what about you?

Let me explain. Up until five years ago I really didn't like those crazy songs that had actions to them. I was too inhibited. I suppose that really is not true. I really did like the songs, and I envied those who could enter into them so freely, but because I was so uptight I tended to dismiss them by saying they were dumb.

Up until a few years ago I did not think it was O.K. for me to cry and show my feelings. At the tennis court this summer we were watching a match. A little boy of three or four was standing on a stone retaining wall when he fell off onto a wooden sidewalk. He really didn't hurt himself, but he was frightened and had banged his chin and his tummy. As his mother comforted him one of the ladies beside him said, "That's a good little soldier. You didn't cry." I found it very difficult not to rebuke her for that kind of inhibiting statement, because I wanted the child to know that it is all right to have feelings and express them appropriately. It was O.K. for him to cry, and I wanted him to know it.

In the past I've been inhibited to the point that I've been unable to ask for help, because as a clergyman I thought I was supposed to have all the answers.

I could not tell people I was hurting and afraid and lonely because Christians, and especially clergy, are not supposed to be afraid and lonely or hurting. I was really out of touch with my feelings.

So for me, and for you too if you are like I was, the story of the children and their special qualities can be very discouraging and maybe even threatening. How can we enter into the kingdom of God and receive his gift if we aren't like little children? Nicodemus asked Jesus, "How can a grown man be born again?"

We might want to say, "Lord, how can middle-agers, or indeed anyone, change to become like little children again? How can we have the qualities of being spontaneous and free and trusting and open so we can receive the gift of the kingdom of God?"

I would like to suggest three things to you from

my own experience of these past few years that may enable us to be more childlike.

I have just been reading *The Undiscovered Self* by Carl Jung, and he expresses there great concern for the individual because we are living in a scientific-statistic-oriented society. Our modern society lives on statistics, and when we begin to reduce people to statistics—which we have already started to do—we begin to blur the individual and his or her uniqueness.

That can happen in the church too. Belonging to the church can be a statistical experience. The year book of any church or denomination shows how the people of God can be reduced to a listing of statistics: number of births, deaths, baptisms, confirmations, dollars and cents, etc. When that begins to happen, it not only blurs the individual's worth, but also wipes out the excitement of the Good News that God has come to each of us, that the kingdom of God is a personal gift offered to you and me.

The biblical message is one of grace, which is the unearned, undeserved, unmerited love of God for each one of us, and if we believe that claim by faith, not only does our view of the world begin to change, but a change begins to take place within us as the Holy Spirit manifests in us the fruits of the Spirit: love and joy and peace and goodness and faithfulness. When these qualities begin to appear we become, I believe, more open and transparent and trusting—the very qualities Jesus says we need to enter into the kingdom of God.

So the first thing I need to remember, if I am going to recapture these childlike qualities, is that God has reached out to me, not only to change my relationship to him, but to begin the healing of my own self and my relationship to others.

When I became a Christian it was just God and me. It was very personal. I had no sense of belonging to a community. Everything that I did in the church in Ottawa, whether it was Sunday school, working on the session, prayer, devotions, or Bible studies, was done simply to make better, to shore up, to make more secure my relationship with God. It was a lonely existence. I was trying to be a Robinson Crusoe Christian. It didn't work. Only in these past four or five years have I discovered that I belong to all of you in the family of God and that you belong to me. Oh, I knew about community before as a pastor, but it was an institutional, cerebral kind of experience. I was the shepherd and they were my flock. But I need this feeling of belonging to you in the community to confirm to myself that I have value and worth, and that I don't have to try to earn God's love or yours.

Yesterday I was reading a devotional book in which the author asked me to try to think of three people who believed I had value and worth just for being me. The three persons I thought of were members of a small church which I belong to here in Hamilton. Being able to come up with their names really felt good.

When people love us in this way (as imperfect as the expression of it may be), and we *dare* to believe it, we start to let down our defenses, to admit our fears, to confess our pride, to drop our masks and to begin to become what Jesus says we must be in order to enter into the kingdom of God. That's true. It is for me, and for every Christian. So community is an integral part of my change.

One of the things that I've learned is that a lot of Christians do not love themselves very much. That may sound strange, but it is true. Somewhere, somehow, we have got the message of

Jesus turned around. Jesus says that the great commandment is to love God with all of your heart and your mind and your soul and your neighbor *as yourself.* Most Christians, for some reason or other, says Walter Trobish in his book *Love Yourself* have translated that to read, "Love your neighbor instead of yourself," but that is not what Jesus said.

Many people get very nervous when you talk about loving yourself. It sounds as if you are being self-centered and egotistical. But loving yourself can have two meanings, says Trobish. One is self-preserving and healthy, and the other is self-destructive. The reason loving yourself is so important, he points out, is that it is the guide that Jesus gave us for loving our neighbor. If you don't love yourself, you can't love your neighbor. Loving ourselves is also important because loving ourselves allows us to let others love us and minister to us and care for us. That is how we grow in the Lord. In order for people to care for us it is *necessary* for us to become open about our needs. When we do we begin to trust and allow ourselves to be dependent and to experience one aspect of the childlike qualities of which Jesus speaks. If we don't love ourselves, we have trouble letting others care for us because we don't think we are worthy of their care.

Now people can love themselves selfishly or selflessly. Self-love in a positive sense is the basis of selflessness. It is only when we have accepted ourselves that we can become free of ourselves and love others. Jesus, says Trobish, knew who he was, and his self-acceptance allowed him to turn his attention to others.

So often because of our misconceptions of what constitutes real Christian modesty and humility, we ward off expressions of love and praise and affirmations that would build our self-esteem. After a Sunday service, people sometimes say, "That was a great sermon." In the past, I would often reply, "Praise the Lord." That may sound very spiritual and sometimes it may have been appropriate, but for me it was really a way of warding off praise, of deflecting it, because I really could not handle it. Now when people are affirming I am able to say, "Thank you." And when praise is directed to my sermons, I find myself able to say, "I enjoyed it too." And that feels good.

So when I love myself in a healthy way, I can begin to demonstrate those childlike qualities of trust and care and dependency and openness of which Jesus spoke because I am secure. I can risk it. But I need you and the community to help me love myself in order to risk demonstrating these qualities.

So, grace, community, and self-love are for me important ingredients. They allow me to begin to be the kind of person who is trusting, open, dependent, free, and therefore able to receive the kingdom of God and be blessed. And that feels good.

Life Is on the Patio

Karl Olsson in his recent book, *Meet Me on the Patio,* talks about how we relate to each other. To illustrate his point, he uses a picture of two high-rise office buildings (called the Twin Towers) which face each other and are connected on the street level by a patio. The one tower represents you, and the other tower represents me. The foundation of the twin towers consists of our common human experiences and needs. It is Karl's contention that we often miss meaningful, personal interaction on the patio by trying to relate to one another from the upper levels of our tower. These upper levels represent things like talent, skills, credentials, and status. While a certain communication is possible between people of similar attributes, it tends to produce an association rather than a relationship. In order for us to relate to one another in a deeply human way, we need to take the elevator down to the patio and meet one another there. That, says Karl, is what the incarnation is all about.

"He became like man and appeared in human likeness. He was humble and walked the path of obedience to death—his death on the cross" (Philippians 2:7*b*-8 TEV).

Coming down to the patio and interacting at the level of our common humanity can be a painful process. If you think pain is a bad thing, then you will avoid the patio and stay in your tower. But I believe that meeting on the patio is the way to experience reality, and, painful or not, I want to be there.

The other day I was reading the familiar story of Zacchaeus in Luke 19:1-10, and I realized that it is a patio story with which I can relate in many ways.

If you remember the story there is Zacchaeus, the crowd, and Jesus. The disciples may have been there, but we don't know. And if we take a moment to think about the various feelings that are present, it adds a great deal to our ability to get into the story and make it ours.

As I thought about it I realized that here was a tremendous range of feeling. Zacchaeus, I am sure, was experiencing the desire to be a different person, the excitement of seeing this new teacher who might help him, frustration because of his height, inferiority because he did not measure up to Jews' spiritual laws, perhaps some superiority because of his wealth, and then, of course, surprise and joy when Jesus saw him and invited himself to dinner.

The feelings in the crowd must have been kaleidoscopic too. They were excited, curious, expectant, hopeful, surprised, disappointed, angry, judgmental, smug, and self-righteous.

And Jesus! I am sure he was feeling a lot of different emotions too. He must have been glad to see the crowds. He could sense their excitement and expectancy. He would have been sensitive to Zacchaeus in a particular way, and he must have felt good when he invited Zacchaeus to come down and Zacchaeus responded so quickly. Jesus must have shared his enthusiasm and his hope. I am sure he, too, rejoiced when Zacchaeus acted in such a responsible, feeling kind of way.

Well, when I become aware of all those feelings as well as the facts, I can begin to own the story in a very personal kind of way. It is obvious that the crowd and Zacchaeus were not on very good terms. They were not meeting on the patio. Zacchaeus was a minor bureaucrat. He had the status of a government official. He was chief tax collector, and Luke says he was rich. So it is my guess that Zacchaeus related to the crowd out of his tower, probably at the level of status and role. He would tend to look down on the crowd as not being very important, except to the extent that they paid their taxes.

But the crowd were tower people too. They did not have his worldly position or wealth, yet they were in their tower in the role of righteous people and looking down, I am sure, on Zacchaeus for not being as spiritual as they were and, therefore, not as acceptable to God.

I think we can infer from Zacchaeus' action that he wanted to change, to come down from his tower as he came down from the tree. In fairness, the crowd might have been open to change too, but Luke does not give us that impression. When Jesus came along and saw Zacchaeus, he did not tell him about the twin towers and the patio because Karl's book had not yet been written. But by his affirmation of Zacchaeus, I believe that Jesus was in fact inviting him to take the elevator and come down to the patio. And he did. In fact, I think he took an express elevator because Luke says that "he made haste and came down" (verse 6).

Zacchaeus was no sooner on the ground than he began to relate in a new way. He was no longer dealing out of his strength and power and wealth. He was Zacchaeus the man, confessing his dishonesty, wanting to make restitution, asking for forgiveness, and seeking acceptance. He was open, honest, vulnerable, and account- able. It was a whole new ball game for Zacchaeus. He was on the patio. Jesus affirms his new style by saying, "Today salvation has come to this house since he is also a son of Abraham" (verse 9). That verse has always seemed so theological, so much like the Old Testament, that I could never quite own it or identify with it. But now as I read it, it sounds like a strong

110

affirmation by Jesus of Zacchaeus' action in coming down from his tower to the patio.

I don't know about you, but I didn't respond to Jesus' invitation to come to the patio so quickly. It took me eight years, and I have since wondered why it took so long. It seems to me that part of the problem was that, unlike Jesus, who spoke to Zacchaeus at the point of his *felt* need, my initial invitation to come to the patio was more a formal declaration of need than any *felt* need. For eight years I was *told* that I was a sinner separated from God who needed to repent and start afresh under the management of Jesus Christ. It took eight years for my head to accept that theological definition of my need. I have been wondering lately if those who presented Jesus to me could have presented him at a point of my *felt* need. If so, then perhaps, like Zacchaeus, I could have responded more quickly. Well, of course, I can't live on what-ifs, but maybe the story of Zacchaeus tells us something very important about the way we present Jesus to people.

We can't read too much into the story. I would like to be able to tell you that the crowd finally came down to the patio, and everyone lived happily ever after together, but I don't think that

Luke suggests that. I'd like to say that Zacchaeus' family, his friends, the disciples, and Jesus rejoiced in his action, but I am not sure of that either. My guess is that his family may have been embarrassed by his public confession and that they may have felt threatened by the way he gave away his money in order to make restitution. His friends may also have been uncomfortable with the new Zacchaeus. So, perhaps all we can safely say is that Jesus rejoiced, and maybe his disciples were accepting too.

The exciting thing is that from now on Zacchaeus' role and status and wealth would not be the means by which he would relate to people. Rather, he would be leading out from his weakness and need, as well as from his gifts.

I want to quickly add that if Zacchaeus was like me, than there would be times when he would want to return to his tower because it would be safer and less threatening and less vulnerable. But even if he gave in to such fears, he would eventually return to the patio because that is where the most meaningful relationships are to be found.

I find it easy to relate to Zacchaeus, as a husband, for instance. Just before leaving on a three-week trip a few months ago, I was talking to Isobel about the children, and among other things, I laid down the law to our two youngest girls about their piano practicing. I was leaving Isobel to be an enforcer, a negative role, one she does not enjoy. Before our conversation was over I began to feel defensive, and I went silent. There I was, leaving town for three weeks, thinking how nice it would be to cuddle up to Isobel that night. No way. We were there, on opposite sides of the bed with four feet of empty sheets in between. The next day, when Isobel took me to the airport, I told her that I really couldn't stand leaving this way, so we talked for a short time, then she said, "Have a good time, if you can." And I left.

Well I can tell you I was in my tower, feeling very insecure and angry, and determined to stay there because it was safer. When I got to Calgary there was a letter from Isobel which was affirming, caring, and in effect an invitation to come down to the patio so we could deal with the unresolved feelings, and that felt good, and we did.

I can also empathize with Zacchaeus as a pastor, because for many years I related to my congregation from the tower of status and role and credentials. I was the Shepherd. I was Mr. Spiritual. I was Reverend Angel. It was really an association, not a relationship.

The father role is one of my favorite tower places, especially if I am feeling insecure. I don't know what it is like in your house, but we like to have some measure of neatness. So to achieve that we ask the children to make their beds and keep their rooms reasonably tidy. I should probably admit that in this area we have been singularly unsuccessful.

The other day I asked Paul to make his bed before going to school. He didn't. I was not surprised. After school, I asked him again, and he didn't move. By that time I was getting very angry. So in my usual way, I went to the kitchen where Isobel was making supper and told her of my frustration and anger. She said, "I'll speak to Paul." When she did, he stormed upstairs mumbling something about the old man because he knew where the order had originated.

As I lay in bed that night I recognized how angry and resentful I was feeling toward Paul and that I would have to be the one to relinquish those feelings because I was the one responsible for how I felt.

The next day I had, for me at least, a great insight (for which I thank the Lord)! I began to see that part of my anger toward Paul was caused by my need to be obeyed. When he paid no attention, he pushed the I-must-be-obeyed button in me. I began to see that if I continued to focus on me then the need to be obeyed would be intensified, and Paul and I would be on a heavy collision course. But if I were to focus on Paul and his need for acceptance during these uncertain adolescent years that our relationship could be maintained and might come out the other side still intact. Now I must make it clear that I do not condone disobedience. But I was experiencing the difference between obedience that is appropriate between a father and a son, and obedience that is necessary to fulfill a need in me, the father.

I also realized that whenever I had read Ephesians 6:1-4 the first thing I noticed was the part which says, "Children obey your parents." I was never really aware of, nor did I really understand verse 4, which says, "Fathers do not provoke your children to anger!" *Now* I know

115

what that really means. If I had insisted on Paul's making his bed *in that context* (of my need to be obeyed), it would have been an act of provocation on my part.

There is a place for the role of parent, don't misunderstand, but laying a "heavy" on children out of a need to be obeyed is not fulfilling the parental role as I understand it. I needed to come to the patio and be known as a person, and then I could better fill my role as father.

The good news in the Zacchaeus story for me is that Jesus not only invites Zacchaeus and me to come down to the patio and be human and be known, but, as Karl says, he has taken the elevator before us. That is what the gospel is all about. The Word of God has become flesh and dwells among us. It was risky and painful, but it was God's way. He chose to meet us on the patio in order to offer us reconciliation and wholeness and salvation. And he not only invites us to come to the patio, but precedes us.

By faith, I believe in the constancy and dependability of God. That faith, and his promises make it possible for me to risk coming to the patio and meeting you there.

I Haven't Blown It

There is a Canadian Christian television
program whose ad says "100% Living with Jesus
Christ." For some reason that statement pushes a
"guilt button" in me. There was a time when that
kind of promise would have excited me—100
percent living! Wow! It sounds super. Fantastic!
Maybe it's my middle-age, but after twenty-eight
years in the Christian life, I have decided that
100 percent living as a Christian, whatever that
means, is just not for real. It is oversell of the
worst kind.

Several years ago I discovered Second

Corinthians 12:9. It is that part of Paul's letter that speaks of the sufficiency of God's grace. It is a superb statement of faith. It was and is very important to me. It became a sort of theme verse for my life. I got so excited that I wrote a hymn about it. But I was doubly blessed. I not only heard about the grace of God with my ears, I felt it in my stomach a few years later, when I was loved by some Christian brothers and sisters before I had proved what a neat guy I was.

And then the New Beginnings Conference took place!

Two years ago Ralph Osborne and I dreamed about a conference where people from local churches would come together with some front-line leaders to encourage and equip the participants to go home and begin to reproduce the relational life-style in their local churches. For me, the local congregation is where it all has to happen, so if we could enable that process by a conference it would be a dream fulfilled.

I became so excited about the conference and the leadership that I began to see people lined up ten deep to get in. We might even have to hire another person at the office to take care of all the registrations. Two weeks before the conference it

118

became clear that people were not lining up, and 150 started to look good. Well, the conference was all I could have imagined in terms of content and leadership and response, but we lost about $3,500. What was God doing? We had tried to be sensitive to the Holy Spirit. So how could we end up this way?

A few days before the conference I was really down. That is an understatement; I felt rotten. Where was the sufficiency of grace of which I spoke? It became clear to me that I had an interpretation of God's grace that you will not find in any biblical commentary. It goes something like this: "God's grace is sufficient when things are going swell, but when they are rotten, forget it."

I realized how much I needed to "make it" with people, with the leadership of the conference, and with the members of my board. But "making it" would mean a large registration and a financially sound conference. Well, I decided that I had blown it again. There was not much 100 percent Christian living in that experience.

And the trouble is that this kind of on-again, off-again state of faith happens over and over again. Awhile back, as I began my day with devotions I asked Christ to be the Lord of my mind, my eyeballs, my ears, and my mouth. I then proceeded into the day with great confidence. Like Peter, I had given my life to the Lord with no conscious reservation, but before the next twenty-four hours had passed the cock had crowed three times.

At lunch Isobel and I sat down to talk about a summer camp program which she had thought a great deal about. Before the conversation was over I had reduced her to tears. At four o'clock when Paul came home from school, I nailed him. He had asked me to mail some thirty letters for him to various scientific communities requesting information about UFO's. The problem was that he had not sealed any of the letters, so I had to lick all thirty of them. That set the stage for an encounter over supper during which he was sent to his room.

At noon the next day I was sitting with Nancy as she practiced the piano. She kept making the same dumb mistake over and over again. My reaction was sufficient to reduce her to tears.

So you see, within the space of twenty–four hours I had left battered bodies all over 66 Fairmount Aveue, in spite of the fact that I had committed my life to the Lord. In that one day I had denied the Lord in three relationships. So I had blown it again! But did I? Remember when Jesus had just eaten the final supper with the disciples and washed their feet. He has given them a new commandment—to love one another as he has loved them. In the midst of the conversation Jesus tells the disciples that he is going away and that they cannot come with him. Peter does not understand. He would go anywhere with Jesus, and he says, "Lord, I would lay down my life for you." Although Jesus knows that Peter will soon deny him, he does not put Peter down with "You don't know what you are saying Peter." He accepts the expressed loyalty and love and devotion.

And look at what Jesus does. He tells Peter that he is going to deny him. Yes, but then he says, "Let not your hearts be troubled; believe in God, believe also in me" John 14:1). I used to think that these words were reserved for funerals to comfort the bereaved. That, at least, is where I have always used them. But William Temple in his *Readings in St. John's Gospel* says that the concluding words of chapter 13, where Jesus says, "You will deny me," and the opening words of chapter 14, "Let not our hearts be troubled," should go together. "Let not your hearts be troubled" is spoken by Jesus to comfort his disciples who have been made aware that they are going to fall flat on their faces and deny the Lord. But more than that. I believe that Jesus was saying, in effect, that their failure must not become a cause for their despair or isolation from God and from each other.

Jesus is not condemning them for their failure and clay-footedness. Neither is he condoning. He is telling them that this is part of the process of discipleship. We shall fail and fall. We can expect that. It is part of being human. It is part of being changed from one degree of glory to another, and it is O.K. In other words, the Christian life is not 100 percent performance all the time.

Maybe it is more realistic to say that 35 percent consistency is what we can expect. Maybe someone has just been laying a "trip" on us when they talk about 100 percent living with Jesus Christ. Maybe real Christian living is high moments of devotion and low moments of failure and frustration, and all the struggle in between!

The trouble is that even in writing this I am feeling uncomfortable and guilty. I am feeling that maybe I am not spiritual enough or that I have not prayed enough or that I have not read my Bible sufficiently. That may all be true. And yet when I think about it, even those whom I know to be very spiritual are also inconsistent when they are willing to be honest about it. They are struggling just as I. Maybe it is time that I accept an enormous change in my thinking which says to me, "Following Jesus Christ is a very uncertain thing. So stop trying to live up to the expectations of others and any dictum that holds you in bondage. Accept the fact that you have this treasure in an earthen, clay-footed vessel."

I am realizing that the ad "100 percent Living with Jesus Christ" has that "be perfect" ring about it and that is the biggest "trip" that was ever laid on us Christians. Even the most conservative commentators make it clear that the word "perfect" in Matthew 5:48 is a misleading translation of *teleios* and is largely responsible for the erroneous doctrine of "perfectionism." Men can never be perfect as God is perfect; and Jesus himself taught that at best,

123

when men have done everything possible, they are unprofitable servants who have just barely done their duty. "Be ye perfect" (Matthew 5:48) really means showing kindness to all men without exception, just as God makes no exceptions.

Oswald Chambers in his classic devotional book, *My Utmost for His Highest* says,

"It is a snare to imagine that God wants to make us perfect specimens of what He can do; God's purpose is to make us one with Himself. The emphasis of holiness movements is apt to be that God is producing specimens of holiness to put in His museum. If you go off on this idea of personal holiness the dead-set of your life will not be for God, but for what you call the manifestation of God in your life. It can never be God's will that I should be sick. If it was God's will to bruise His own Son, why should He not bruise you? The thing that tells for God is not your relevant consistency to any idea of what a saint should be, but your real vital relation to Jesus Christ and your abandonment to Him whether you are well or ill. Christian perfection is not, and never can be, human perfection."

Several days after speaking at a conference in Barrie, Ontario, I received a beautifully lettered prayer from a member of the audience. It was the prayer of a *slave* referred to by Gert Behanna in her record "God Isn't Dead." It says:

> O Lord, I aint what I wanta be;
> O Lord, I aint what I oughtta be;
> and Lord, I aint what I'm gointa be;
> But thanks Lord,
> I aint what I usedta be!

And that says it for me.

I am changing. I am in a process. I am not the same as I used to be. There are and will be times of reversion and slipping and falling, but praise the Lord, there will also be times for new touches of the grace of God.